Winter Poems
Along the Rio Grande

Jimmy Santiago Baca

Winter Poems
Along the Rio Grande

A New Directions Book

The quotation by Thomas Merton is from *Raids on the Unspeakable*, Copyright © 1964 by The Abbey of Gethsemani, published by New Directions, used by permission.

Book design by Sylvia Frezzolini Severance
Manufactured in the United States of America.
New Directions Books are printed on acid-free paper.
First published as New Directions Paperbook 987 in 2004
Published simultaneously in Canada by Penguin Books Canada Limited.

Library of Congress Cataloging-in-Publication Data

Baca, Jimmy Santiago, 1952–
Winter poems along the Rio Grande / Jimmy Santiago Baca.
    p. cm.
"A New Directions Book."
ISBN 0-8112-1575-X (alk. paper)
1. Rio Grande Valley—Poetry.   2. Rio Grande—Poetry.
3. Winter—Poetry.   4. Nature—Poetry.   I. Title.
PS3552.A254W56 2004
811'.54—dc22
                                        2003025679

New Directions Books are published for James Laughlin
by New Directions Publishing Corporation,
80 Eighth Avenue, New York, NY 10011

for Esai

Winter Poems
Along the Rio Grande

When the poet puts his foot in that ever-moving river,
poetry itself is born out of the flashing water.
In that unique instant, the truth is manifest to all
who are able to receive it.

—Thomas Merton

1.

Now and then a bicyclist on the bosque path
flies past me and I stop, quickly get out of the way,
watch him, outfitted in full gear, expensive sunglasses and
                                                            gloves,
shiny white racing helmet and black skin-tights,
          then I'm back on the path again
          looking around for signs to connect me
to the navel of the universe in the tree-trunk knot.

A small yellow spider
teaches the craft of writing,
its amazing web teaches
life is not
a rehearsal for living someday—
          I live now.

My surprise discovering
the laughter that rises in my mistakes.
Create your own Spring season
the herons tell me migrating north in the sky—
          I stop to watch them,
          asking my Creator for insight
          into their hearts, *let me be a blue heron,* I whisper,
          and for an instant
          each fine tendril of my feathered tendons
          is a shrine-offering to the light.

I follow behind others
of the Wing Tribe, wing-bowers
infused with an abundance
          of praising the Great Will, the Great Truth
          each wing beat of theirs,

                   pushes my legs one in front of the other
carrying me toward my own being re-feathered
in white, in black, in brown, in red.

My breathing is not my own,
my hands belong to the wind,
my legs to this path,
my patterns of living and familiar routines become twigs I crush,
the brush and trees become my community, and here, on a
                                        branch I pass
          I see myself perched on the side of a tree clinging
                                                  to bark
tapping out another temple in the bark
          a sanctum for a small heart the size of a walnut
          worshipping with each beat
          the up-suck energy in the roots
          the dirt-food, water-food, air-food.

So I run, I breathe,
shattering my self-centeredness
against each tree, bush, bird, horse and field I sight,
looking all around me—
          at the leaf-covered path,
          up at the towering leafless tree branches,
          the blue sky space between each bough
          is the insight I search for in these crowd-colliding days:
a blue space where there is nothing but the sound of silence
harmonizing its beautiful vowels into my soul,
pouring it in my veins,
forcing me over the top of myself
over the brim of my body
into the air.

     I stop before a thick-trunked short-leaning close-to-the-
                                        ground tree

to pray, a place I've made my shrine,
and exhausted from the five mile run
I bow to the east, asking the Light to guide me and illuminate
my path,
I turn south asking the Darkness to befriend me and teach me
vigilance,
I turn west to my ancestors, thank them for carrying messages
to the Creator,
then north, where I pray to the great Bear for healing and
moral strength.

2.

Today, running along the river,
        dead leaves cling
        to cathedral cottonwood branches,
        snap in the gusty breeze,
        give a crisp hiss . . .
A wafer thin wind spades up
loose dust from the path,
and above me,
gray leaves clash soft in towering boughs;
        sounds
        that might be heard in the silent yard
        of a monastery
        like the sandaled steps of monks
        praying, walking
        over the swept yard,
        walking and praying.

I run, beneath the winter leaves
when right ahead of me at the turn,
        a plump pheasant
        white ring neck, gray-black mottled feathers,
        green phosphorescent head
          scurries into the dry brush,
        clashing like rosaries in the sleeves of nuns
        hurrying to the chapel for evening mass.

        I jog on. A hawk swoops out
and vanishes into the tree tops toward the river.
        Black crows.
Clean swept dirt.
Then at the end of the path,
turning, heading north, I worry over the love
I have for this woman. Then I see seven pairs

of mallards burst up in fright at my sudden appearance,
and I think how they mate for life and beyond them,
poised on the ditch bank, with such regal bearing,

a blue heron . . .

It's then I hear a voice,
a crystal shining icicle clear voice,
cold water but made of sound,
tells me, keep my connection to the spirits strong,
keep my work spiritual,
stay connected to the Creator,
and all my worries will be answered in time.

Ah, it is a good run . . .

3.

This morning, more than ever,
I feel a sense of strength, not the kind that flexes
biceps and poses for the mirrored ahhs.
      I reap
a satisfaction in my heart
and with a certain gratitude
wear the scars of those who have criticized me.
I pray each morning to the spirits to carry my prayers
to the Creator,
      but I want more than that to happen,
I not only want my prayers answered,
I pray that I become stronger,
more sure of the journey ahead of me,
not succeeding where others could not
but to be more honest in my words, more so with my actions,
more thoughtful each day,
      following the whispered signs from spirits
that lead me forth, in the will of the Creator.

      I wake up each morning
        while others are still dreaming
          and mindfully
          say my prayers
asking for the woman I love to understand me
to return to her ways with me
      to wake with me
      pray beside me
      as I wake to my prayers,
          as I wake to this growing strength to love,
          as I learn to live consciously, open my eyes
to see, to care, to share this strength,
to embrace, and take

her to see that red-tailed hawk I saw yesterday
at the river
how I had never seen a hawk so close to me before,
as if it intended to fly low enough for me to lightly caress
its red tail feathers
the kindling color of coals in the dark
flickering in the breeze like embers—
    I felt its feathered heat
    a dream I had
of a light that came to me
illuminating itself as my father,
as the world I must strive for
and this light,
        this exalted glowing eruption of light
I have in me
growing daily
in measure to my own fearless strength to grow with it
and I do on faith—

        Creator, grant my wishes
        hear my prayers.
        I pray to you, surrender to you,
        allow me to serve you
        honor you
        welcome you in my life
    and let that glow, that heat, that light
    radiate from my finger tips, my tongue
    my feet, my laughter and my tears.
        Today I pray I am honest in my life
        as was the hawk when it glided above me
        carrying my prayers to you,
        honest as the hawk when its held its wing-spread
                    true on the updraft
                    and its feathers

each tendril, each feather
played the wind like a lover's kisses
against its lover's lips,
holding to the wind like a lover holds a lover's hand
fingers clasped, braiding
each other's fingers
as they walk the journey in faith
that each will be true to the other.

And so I pray I am today as honest
with myself,
with life all around me and below and above me,
with all who I encounter.

4.

The elegance with which,
in the sweetest humility, the
lilac senses the time
        to show itself—
        fights adversity all winter
        coldest nights,
        blowing storms,
clinging to fence posts,
tossed and heaved,
trampled, pecked by crows,
almost eaten by insects,
pummeled by brute heat—
        yet the whole time
        still as a stone-carved Buddha
        meditating,
silently greets the world
in its vow of silence, birth to death alone, in the rain
weaving its being into a nameless red blossom
opening at dawn.

        And its body
                we preserve
                in pages of books,
                that have kept our belief in love,
                next to poetry lines we love so much
                        where we place our dreams
                        for safekeeping
                        from the harmful world
                        that hurts us so much some times,
                                I place this flower.

5.

This morning before we met for coffee I was thinking
of my brother, and others who never made it to live the life
they dreamed,
about our paths, the broken marriages, children we brought forth into
the world,
the Rio Grande where every day I meditate, taking note of the river's
ways,
seeking to learn its wisdom, its methods
the way it lets go, surrenders to each season
what it cherishes most, what makes its life and gives it color,
it releases like a huge loving mother
who
tears a part of her heart out
and offers her laughter and sadness to me
in a lofty sunflower or red leaf.

I was thinking of the Rio Grande as a pair of mother's hands,
not those hands that have
built cities or Olympian hands in
grueling gut-grunging competition
to be the best,
they are mere gnats in a starving mongrel's neck scruff;
but as I sat at the river
it unspun in me a vision of things to come:
from a Serbian leader accused of genocide,
a man choking off his soul to attain his ambitious ends,
carrying a million passengers to their destinations,
to a dark-skinned woman dancing the tango in Buenos Aires
like an insane butterfly in a tropical garden
in a salsa club where the ghosts of poets sit at tables and drink
the air as if it were the most savory liquor,
a Virginia field slumbering in red clay bliss,

woods echoing with frozen, creaking pine trunks
unable to endure their own height,
mountain boulders turning over slowly like bears awakening from
hibernation,
sands in Utah bleeding white dirt
from the betrayals of nuclear waste dumped in them.

Meditating on a mother's hands,
the river in me sings my gratefulness to you and others,
how selfless the river is
when I stop to wonder at a million twigs strewn about the
ground.
I am reduced in the river's presence
to a single note in this orchestra of forest trees,
my voice an unfolding tiny green leaf,
singing of my heart's changing river currents.

And I pray:
let all my sensibilities be the breathworkings of this forest,
let its quiet fire, the invisible tissues of its flame, enter me, bless me, re-molecule
my DNA
to be more it than me,
to be more it than what I want
to be more it than what I desire
to be more it
than what I love,
and in all of that love,
let me rise as a tree,
a flower,
wild grass,
river shrubs and tangled brush.

I celebrate mother's hands,
shape-shifters that heal our wounds

and induce me to be as close to what this river is,
   risk who I am in all I do to recreate me
   molded in mother's river hands
         there to embrace my frail strength
         to push me forth, becoming more the
               river than myself . . .

6.

I watch the river water shift and whirl, wanting my life that way—
 with such grace,
  the current caresses its way forth
  be it stone, branch, dirt island,
  constantly changes and re-creates its passage
  its way around, along, between, bulging and narrowing
  welcoming struggle.

    I've stood here, asking the river's blessings
    a year now,
    holding my heart out to it,
    a heap of broken pieces
    I scatter
    over the silvery effulgence sparkling with sunlight,
    even when it's gray and overcast
    the river shines.
      If I cried right now,
       it would be out of joy,
        for having this river here with me
      I'd cry for making the mistakes I've made,
      for having the faith that tomorrow might be a better day
      and the eagerness to put one foot in front of the other.
The river has taught me
patience—a year I've stood every day to watch it,
pray to it that I connect my present moment
to my origins as it does, that I am connected now
    to my beginnings as it is,
    its source gathers a million beginnings
    gracefully blending and fusing all threads of experience
    and joins them, braids them, into something as beautiful
    as this river now—flowing, connecting
    my snow-melt loneliness, my rain-tears grief, my joyous
                    natural-spring laughter.

And the river has always loved me,
I've come here after drinking all night,
come here after betraying myself and others I've loved,
come here and offered all the shame and guilt to this river,
to take it down river, pouring it out into the Gulf
        of Mexico,
there for the whales to spout it up in the air,
for the dolphins to spin their acrobatic spirals around it,
to cleanse it, joining me
     in their wholeness, their completeness.

I breathe part of its being in me, the water turns to
oxygen that lifts itself up
into the sky, and in Salt Lake City, California, Mexico, New York,
                                  Cape Cod,
New Orleans, San Antonio, Durango, Santa Barbara, Santa Clara,
                                  Portland,
the lovers I've been with appear on the surface of the water
and breathe the air with me,
become part me again and I am part them, we breathe the air
made partly from this water,
    their faces reflected in the water
go by me sparkling down river
nourishing the earth roots,
feeding the sweet tendrils of river grass,
                breathing out the hurt
                breathing in the hope,
as the water, not a single ripple the same, not a solitary one
can be by itself, but all together act in unison
to create this music we call a river.
            I meant to hurt no one
            and give my regret to the river,
            and as the river I too tried to furrow a passage,
        tunnel a way out of sorrow as gracefully as the river does,

shining, offering itself to mallards and Canada geese, hawks,
                                    hummingbirds,
roadrunners,
whose feathers I have found the past year,
collected them in a box
and framed them in designs to give as gifts
to my friends.

And as the river courses down,
me on the banks hypnotized by its silent dance,
I kneel and dab my fingers in it,
           touch water to my lips so what I speak
           will be as true and necessary as water,
           touch my fingers to my breast
           so what I create will be as honest and giving as the water.
Then I pray that the river help me on this day be fully me,
as true as it is to its destiny,
accept fate as it accepts its fate,
know myself as it knows itself and be me as it is it,
to offer myself to my daily task as it indulges freely in its task:
           Allow me, bless me,
           to be as you are, river, on this day
           and as I enter people's lives
           may I enter as you enter the earthen ground
           making a river channel for your expression of love,
           may I express my own,
           speak my words as you communicate yours
           in grass and trees and animals,
           be only what I am on this day and no more,
           offer only what is needed to carry aloft another person's love
           and purpose in life.

I bow before you river, open myself to you,
lay my brown-rag soul on the ground

bare myself, the innermost core, to you
and ask that you wash away the lies,
heal the hurts, teach me again to dance,
to rejoice, as you do, at the small tiny blossom
of an anonymous flower in the weeds.
So now, my footprint on a journey I begin now from your

banks—

I pray
let each succeeding footprint be as true,
let my tracks follow your tracks
doing what we were meant to do,
be as you,
as each of your gestures reflects who you are.

7.

I wake up—a winter silence fills my apartment
with the mystery of life—
>   why here, why now, why me:
>   I wonder what birds are nesting at this cold hour
>   in bushes by the river, hibernating in their feathers.
>   I imagine they
>   do not dream about war,
>   each breath for them is a cleansing baptism of a constantly
>   occurring miracle,
>   each feather tucked snugly to contain warmth
>   purifies each heart
>   that beats to be what it is.

I must tell you that I seek their wisdom,
each day
casually study them as I walk the ditch bank—
they seem to understand there is no death in life,
their serene poise on water
beneath the leafless overhanging branches
is movement toward the center of love.

>   I wonder why I am this man
>   making his coffee this morning
>   wondering about old loves,
>   reading poems, joining the universe each morning through
>   prayer,
>   each day a commemorative ritual
>   to appreciate friends,
>   each day my skin disappears more
>   until I feel transparent,
>   feel an inner glowing heat radiating from me
my life a steaming footprint
melting in the sunrise,

my life glistening frost
shimmering on the bush leaves;
      each a green day of ecstatic life branched out,
      smoldering towards its inevitable death
      that offers its warmth to birds asleep in the bush.

This silence
remembers in its deep dark chords and drums
a life beyond this life,
a beauty beyond this beauty.
      I catch glimpses of eternity sometimes in stray dogs
      meandering down trails by the river.
Sadness and happiness
embrace me as I wake each morning
arriving, a freed prisoner
given a big bear hug by these brothers and sisters
      who do not blame or pity me,
asking only from me to treat life
the same as air treats wings,
dry channels treat water,
spring treats budding leaves.
      If you ask me
      what I believe in
      I say the silence
      this morning, the memory of Dan yesterday
      calling to rave about a book he's reading
      or Ruby last night with the shy look in her brown eyes
      in the kitchen when she introduced me to her
         friend—
      in her own way, in this loving way, in this intimate
      way of hers—
         she fights against the darkness,
         she renounces defeat for the moment,
reaching to a hand, to smile, to embrace,
she becomes the mallard in the bush,

its sensuous eyelids, its form, its silence blending into the silence
of this morning, a flute, a very old flute
playing a very old song in tribute to life,
to the awakening of the heart
to struggle again, to fight again
to believe again.

8.

for Tony & Mildred

As a child I lived in a corner—
I'd place my mat on the floor
padding the wood,
patting down my blankets into a mound-cushion
and I curled up on them, a dog, snuggling into myself,
smelling my own smell, my own hair, my own limbs, my own
                                                    breath—
and because I had all these
I wished the world a good night.
My breath a baby eagle's white emerging talon
scratching the air at the night's vast face of stars and shadows,
I dreamed of
grizzly bears romping in green pastures
and rams on snowcapped
peaks.

As a teenager
I back-packed, clothing
t-shirt and jeans
and ambled in the great prairie,
with the worn out guitar of sadness
over my shoulder,
and sometimes I would strum the sweetest songs
to the grass,
I hailed the wind as savior, reached up and
honored with
both arms
the elm, cedar, and mesquite trees that seldom
gave their voices to me but always, always
patiently
listened, their black birds clapping wings
as I hunkered up stony hills of small
villages

where the people still buried their dead in
capillas,
tiny little chapels,
they would bury their infants in
the dirt
behind the altar
and I would enter, seeking warmth
from the
chill dawn,
and sing to the little baby
who had died from pneumonia.

I knew back then I couldn't leave the guitar anywhere,
because when I left it against a rock,
it would rise, float in the air, lay itself against my shoulder
a horse nuzzling my elbow for sugar cubes
or my heart for songs,
and I sang them,
knowing what I sang was a gift for others,
that I could not keep it,
in the same way my grandma fed strangers in our kitchen
heaping their plates with beans, chile, tortillas
while I knew after they left
we'd be out of food.

As a man,
while staying in a Malibu hotel room and waking up
early
enough to catch the tide
fiercely assault the shore, lashing it with conga-maddened hands,
the waves like a thousand gypsy dancers
shook hips, clapped hands, flung their hair around, sweating
as they swayed their shoulders and undulated their pelvises
in the fiercest storm destroying
moaning orgasm on me,

as if nothing mattered to them,
and nothing mattered to me.
I ran along the shore,
knew in my blood it was a deep blessing,
a calling to sing, a preaching to me
to pass up what others might take from life
and lunge myself into the shore of the openness of each day
and sing as these waves danced for me.

So I carry
this worn guitar now, have for thirty years
from town to town,
from Baltimore's crack-infested tenements,
to New York's Lower East Side where young vatos
strut their pitbulls,
down to El Paso where young lions of Chicanos roam the
streets
filming and writing poetry and drinking and laughing,
and over the years,
along with a robust laughter that always echoes stampeding from
canyons,
there is a sadness that attends my every gesture
shadows every word,
lurks behind each laughter.

I sense it sometimes emerge, hiding in my sleeves and
coloring my cheeks when I'm in the mountains
in a quaint resort town—
I'm coming out of a door onto the cold morning streets
and seeing people in their jackets, cotton caps, clomping in their
boots
over last night's fallen snow,
this sadness observes them through my eyes
and imbues me with compassion

for us—we humans, we people who will always make mistakes,
and just as suddenly,
I am seeing them as children sipping soup from large spoons
their eyes on the soup, avoiding their mother and father
who last night raged from drinking and arguing,
and suddenly the child singer I was in my grandmother's kitchen is
climbing
up on the chair and reaching for the guitar
hanging on a peg-bone of my ribs
and as I walk down the street for my coffee, I am singing, almost
weeping
so that I can't breathe, almost weeping and yet in each
tear is a
smile
a song, a laugh for our benefit,
praising our glory, our reluctance over our heartbreaks
and I sing
as the forest has taught me,
as the mountain in Canones has taught me, as my dear love
has taught me,
as my friends at the Sacred Circle have taught me,
as Efren, Valentin, and others on the basketball court at
the gym
have taught me,
as my dog, Green Sage has taught me,
as my children have shown me—
that there is room for all of us,
and plenty of love to go around,
this is what I sing sitting on the banks of the Rio Grande
watching the current's curling into smooth down flowing
love to
its ending;
that I, like it, am to make islands of my songs
where people who can't swim the width, who aren't as strong

to make the full distance others can,
let my songs become sandbars and small islands where they
can rest,
where the geese migrating south can nest,
where the wild seeds blown in from hundreds of miles away
in the prairies, where other grandmothers this minute
share their food with strangers,
can root, open, sprout the greening of my
gifts
offered up freely beneath the sun,
to all, of every color and spiritual inclination.

All our origins issue from the same great navel of life,
and I am lucky, I have songs
to give away every day.
I never come empty,
I come bearing gifts that I play on this worn out
guitar
made from crooked branches in the bosque, made from dreams
the Rio Grande gave me,
made from mud I stood and prayed on at night
made from brush and rabbits and hawks I've seen
and from the silence in the bosque,
I come offering you the gift of my sadness,
the sand in my wound.
I breathe in and out of injury
in my constant birthing
to renew the edge and cut a winding path,
and keep on it,
keep moving uphill, down through the valley
meeting strangers wherever I go and playing a song for them,
a song as light and whimsical as mother's skirt touching and
bouncing off her calves,
hurrying as mothers do, to attend their loves,
their children, their cooking, their ways of loving.

9.

for Miguel

It would be neat if with the New Year
I could leave my loneliness behind with the old year.
My leathery loneliness an old pair of work boots
my dog vigorously head-shakes back and forth in its jaws,
chews on for hours every day in my front yard—
rain, sun, snow, or wind
in bare feet, pondering my poem,
I'd look out my window and see that dirty pair of boots in the yard.

But my happiness depends so much on wearing those boots.

At the end of my day
while I'm in a chair listening to a Mexican corrido
I stare at my boots appreciating:
all the wrong roads we've taken, all the drug and whiskey houses
we've visited, and as the Mexican singer wails his pain,
I smile at my boots, understanding every note in his voice,
and strangers, when they see my boots rocking back and forth on my
                                               feet
keeping beat to the song, see how
my boots are scuffed, tooth-marked, worn-soled.

I keep wearing them because they fit so good
and I need them, especially when I love so hard,
where I go up those boulder strewn trails,
where flowers crack rocks in their defiant love for the light.

10.

Listening to jazz now, I'm happy
        sun shining outside like it was my lifetime achievement award.
            I'm happy,
with my friend Amy and her dog up in Durango, her emailing
        me this morning
no coon hound ailing yowls
but vibrant I love yous.
            I'm happy,
            my smile a big Monarch butterfly
            after having juiced up some carrots, garlic, seaweed,
            I stroll the riverbank, lazy as a deep cello
in a basement cabaret—
                        smoke, cagney'd out patrons
                        caramel and chocolate women in black
                                    shoulder strap satin dresses,
                        and red high heels.

I'm happy being me this day, like the solo trumpet note trailing off in
                                                a movie
when the man
in the topcoat with turned up collar
turns down a rainy street corner at night
heading to meet the moon,
        and bet his dreams,
        pull out some money and bet his hand,
                    bet that he wins it all, and does;
                    then later, after fried eggs, bacon, hash
                                brown and coffee breakfast,
                feeling lucky—
I write a poem on a napkin and leaves it as a tip
for the waitress, with my phone number.
She calls later,

her name's Amy, lives up in Durango with her dog Simon,
   says she loved the poem,
   and I say I was just feeling blue,
   asking her if maybe later, she'd go for a walk,
     along the river baby,
     'cuz I'm happy
     and feeling a little lucky . . . .

11.

You and me walk by the river.
I think how your words
fit gently into each other like folded feathers
suddenly opening in me an upward flight of joys in my deep quietness.
     You and me
in the bark gnawed by beavers—
they have the most beautiful ivory, yellowed, burnished buckteeth,
tiny skulls I found one day, two of them, shot by a hunter in the back
                              of the head,
their teeth
          were the teeth of your words
          shaving the charred bark away from my fear,
          ashed from past fires,
          and still remembering the hot wind blow,
my fear
leaned, creaked forward and fell,
in the open space of my yearning you.
In this yearning toward sky and sun
          unfolds our beliefs in love,
          in the way I learn,
          in the way I approach you, and agree
               to trust you,
and be your man,
is an awakening of spring rain in my groin,
and a fluttering storm of leaves in my heart.

In the bosque's disarray, chaos rules
yet there is room for every living thing,
where things die, molt back to earth,
     where things crack, give, break, show their fragile strengths

their beautiful humility,
  there is no ego, no complaints, no expectations,
  just what are
the faces of our souls celebrating our brief passage
through life.

12.

        The crook where branches separate
        veering in two directions
                        always the choices
                        that make us vulnerable—
in the tension of opposition, I sing my blues to you mama,
twanging my staunch-legged heart-strings to hee-haw my braying-
                                        mule blues
        of love.

        Where we meet and weep, laugh, eat and sleep,
        where we doubt and pray and hope and forgive,
unites and divides in random balance
        barely clinging—
                        its arrangement,
                        spirit-made connections between us
                        over the years.
A gushing rain-fulfilling giving
of love
open-hearted joy to give to you
who I am
what I have
on the verge of always splitting and breaking in half,
but climbing my love climbing my love
to the sun . . . yeah!

Yeah! Yeah! Yeah!
        Let's clap,
and sing from our cabin porch and call out our names to the sky,
shaking our shoulders, our heads swaying back and forth,
and let
        sunlight re-sage, re-leaf, re-grass
        our bones and hair and flesh
        photosynthesizing
                        our hearts into leaf shivering delight.

13.

This is supposed to be a love poem for Stacy
something beautiful, but that word, beautiful
is insufficient,
     like leaving out salt from tortillas,
won't convey what I have in my heart—
     a lightning dance
broadcasting our frequencies of love
to butterflies, flowers, stars, planets,
fields of green grass.
     What we do detects
          God in the common woman and man,
what we do when we have coffee is balance,
in our small conversations,
the world with infusions of love.

     You and I
     move through the days like bluejays,
     disturbing the sleeping souls
          with radical cries of love,
          with radical wing-flutters of *move move move*
     and *wake up wake up wake up,*
so much of life to live,
so much to step forward into
when we are awake, we are powerful,
and in each of us the drums need to be pounded,
we need to move our souls as we do our hips in a boot-kicking dance,
we need to mouth our words with hymns to the Creator
and silence our cynical finger pointing accusations,
quit taking and start giving,
quit jeering and weep with hands clasping our brother's hands,
our sister's hands, our children's hands
     we need to WAKE UP!

Join our human forces together and sing from the meadows
sing from the cliffs
sing out the backyard, to the fields, to broad expanses of land
fill the empty spaces with our voices
        bringing our love together and under ONE LOVE,
proclaim our lives our own again,
keep the drums beating in ecstatic commitment
        to truth,
        to dashing our lies against the stones in our yard,
        to opening our arms to our children
        to open wide our hands to the sky
and unabashedly and without shame or delay
whirl in our own happiness that we breathe, that we have a chance
to share our life with others, that we can create
community to care for our infirm, our drug abusers, our criminally
                                                        minded,
we can work, we can teach,
bring them—
        accept them,
        sing their coming back to our communities
        sing our coming back to ourselves,
join our bones into one long flute
and sing the ancient tongue songs of love!

14.

You're out by the pool, reading a book,
and the things that go through my mind—
     like last night,
     I woke up at three a.m., to find you crying
     and I hugged and talked with you
     until four a.m., then we slept
          entangled in each other's arms.
In the past,
     I used drugs to ease the dread
     that gripped my stomach, spread through my arms and legs,
     burned in my breast,
pain from the sorrow I couldn't move past,
and if my life were a map you could point blindly
to any spot,
     there'd be pain, pain rivers, pain mountains, pain roads,
a topography of pain ridged, hilled, valleyed,
and posted with No Trespassing signs everywhere,
where old loves smoldered
and promises and dreams moldered in decaying heaps:

     where birds dropped dead from the air,
     dogs curled over in agony and died,
     faces of ex-lovers cringed with bitterness,
     hungry, barefooted children played on the trash heap,
     finding nothing to eat or use except
     refuge from society, refuge from fears that haunted me,
     refuge in the garbage that had accumulated
          from the thousands of times
          I felt pain and instead of moving into it,
          I numbed myself.
Until
     I felt pain invading my body again,

its hands caressing my spine, scratching the inner lining
of my stomach,
    ripping at my body where tendons hold my arms and legs
                                     together,
and I paced for weeks, couldn't write, read, exercise,
couldn't get together with friends,
        had to be alone and I endured the pain
    moved through it,
    feeling lighthearted.

And what happened was I learned to use the pain
to flow out into the world and create
a world through the pain, from the pain, its origins
birthed in the darkness behind my navel
where my sorrow hibernates, where the rejections, the despairs,
where a teeth-gritting straitjacket sadness gathers
its nest for me to hide in, while I used to opt out for days—

Now, I use this pain,
lure it out, tempt it out with possibilities of devouring me,
woo it,
    and when the pain permeates my entire body
    I feel now as if the Universe has aligned itself
    to direct all its energies toward me,
    and from that dark, infinite hole behind my navel
    instead of seeking refuge from the world there,
    from that horrible void of complete de-creation and non-
                                existence,
    where pain afflicts me like a thousand angry wasps attacking
                                  my face,
    in that moment, when my heart is shocked
    by a thousand volts of killing energy,
    when my face scatters itself into pieces all floating in different
                                directions

when my hands fall off, my legs crumple under me and I can't

walk

and I lose all capacity for language,
cannot speak, only stare out the window
        wishing death upon myself, wishing my life over,
wishing I'd never breathed a single breath
and I secretly curse my fate, damn my destiny
that is an endless series of failures and doom-days,
when that moment looms over me, fills the sky, inhabits the hour
with screeching madness that screams in my ears,
    I face it,
            I motion it closer to me,
            I defy it, challenge it,
then in the ensuing days, I mold the pain,
forge it in my determined hands,
wrestle it down, pin it in the fires that scorch my heart,
until it slowly turns into a book of poems, a novel, a collection of

stories,

until I find myself out at midnight
        with other like-minded gypsies
    curing their pain through work,
    sleepily working their visions alongside mine.

15.

I haven't been to the river in days and I feel
        sad.

These last few days
my spirit has been thirsty
but the days are cotton cloths
in my mouth—
        going to the river
        is drinking
        a cup of fresh water.

I've started smoking again, inhaling the smoke
that swirls softly on the air
like past lovers' voices who call me on the phone,
each puff from my cigarette inhaled
is one of their voices—
        fearful Stacy, lamenting her love,
        unable to move forth from her terror,
        loving me with every gasp of breath,
love me woman, love me woman,
I inhale you.
        What a wonderful and open-hearted woman,
        inviting me as her partner to dance in the universe,
love me woman love me woman
I inhale you.
        Dark, sensuous angel, ready to fling her life
        into my life, offers me her sweet lips and dancer's
hands,
love me woman love me woman
I inhale you.
        You
        were an unplanned miracle, unexpected

dreams that profoundly affected me,
initiated me into my delight of being
in the lovely shape of a female body.

I've shared with you
various moments of blinding love,
a grainy freedom of emotion from Billie Holiday's throat,
the pig's mud sty grunting up mud-love, horse-froth,
                where I devoured your ass, your legs, your breasts,
your
nipples,
                where I consumed your heart with a feverish appetite
                wave upon wave of your stormy love.
You took my soul and wrapped it around you like a sheet,
walked out into the forest with your voice my voice,
                your heart my heart
                your naked hungering my naked hungering
                your wet sex my wet sex,
                        lost, not knowing where to turn.

Each day we breathe we practice loving each other.
You are waking up now, maybe reading a book at your bedside,
looking out the window,
you are not alone, you are not separate—
I sing to you from here, from this corner of life,
I see you unfold the Sunday morning paper and look for our
                                                    horoscopes,
I see you nursing our infant, looking down into our infant's face.
I see you gaze off, a look in your eye
searching in the horizon for me.

                We fuse our souls together
                and when my voice asked for love
                my voice was missing the other half

37

and combined we made the story true, we made the
dream real,
we made each other real, our many selves
blended into each other,
perfectly,
we came together and became one—

so this morning
I swirl cigarette smoke rings from my mouth
sending you my love from this chair, this desk, this moment,
I love you,
     as I move into the airy realm of hours
     remembering you,
     watching as our love loses its ring, its circle,
     fading into air.

16.

I run down the path thinking
how you assume
I can be easily seduced by money
   and little do you know
how I enjoy being alone, in my poverty
I am trying to be like the fields I gaze on my run everyday,
always open and inviting and offering themselves
to migrating cranes and Canada geese.

I am trying to be serene as the gray decomposing leaves
I tread everyday
     how I yearn with all my soul
     to erase the boundaries
     between tree leaf and my flesh.

In Malibu, last week, all night and day,
the ocean splashed up on the balcony:
old grandmother's hands embracing my dreams,
and then the big black boulders on the beach at dawn
as if the waves and rocks
were family members gathering for a long-awaited reunion.

As the ebb and rise arrive predictably,
I am trying to believe in commitment
to one woman again—
   omanagain
    omanagain,
     the word as sounded above
     is as if
     I am giving birth to my child
     through my belly button
     omanagain
     omanagain.

The river teaches me that within
its wild boundaries are commitments—
      I've come here to run
      during rain, snow, wind, cold evenings and hot afternoons,
      breathing its dirt into my lungs
      its green into my nostrils
      breathing it through my eyes, my fingers, my eye-lashes
                           and hair,
      my finger and toenails, a God breathing me forth
                    to its desired end.

          I'm not like
writers who live in
half addresses,
halving their lives between two jobs, halving their dreams
      with hours owned by others,
      days sold for what others might like,
      years gone to the highest bidder,
      and a few handshakes and back-slaps over coffee
      at the Farmers' Market.

      I want to honor and keep this small voice my river gave me.
      One windy afternoon the river placed sand grains in my
                   mouth and said
      sing the ant song,
      one morning I found a blue heron feather floating in the
                     ditch
      and the ditch water said sing the blue feather song,
      and one afternoon the light gave me its sun-song.
The river never taught me to assume, but to watch,
listen, honor the path it travels—
and doing so it promises that one day my heart
      will be a tree in its forest.

17.

Yes, it's true, LA was clearer to me this time—
    I wasn't that young man
    Limoed to Hollywood mansions
eating at fine restaurants
stripping off short skirts and tight blouses
of a different actress every week,
wooed by producers' seven cities of gold promises,
going from a red Converse sneakers, faded jeans, and t-shirt poet,
to Armani, Gucci shoes and Rolex watch wearing screenwriter,
        'til one night
            sitting in a Westwood restaurant,
suddenly overwhelmed with self-loathing,
I rose—
    "I gotta get out of here," I said, and departed.
    And I left
    that cigar-smoking producer at Universal Studios
    sitting in his office,
    left my agent waiting for my call,
    swearing
    I was finished as a writer.

    And I rode out of LA
    driving all night to get back to my river,
        where this morning,
            my soul soars among the treetops
            a red-tailed hawk
            gliding over treetops,
      my soul's wing spread wide and strong,
      my purpose clear as the blue sky,
      my mission certain as the sun this morning.

    At the river
    each day I stand in prayer

pray for light to illuminate my path,
pray for darkness to teach me vigilance,
pray for my ancestors to guide me,
pray to the bear for healing and strength.
These powers
in the bosque
under looming cottonwoods
beside the Rio Grande's lazy waters
recover my soul's voice,
reclaim my role among the rabbits, roadrunners,
lizards
hawks, eagles, horses, coyotes, and catfish,
humble me to my own worth,
following the protocol of the forest
as I shed my flesh,
become a tree, my arms the unruly growl of tree
trunks,
my laughter the bank mud
engraved with paw and claw prints.

18.

The Rio Grande bosque on the verge of bursting forth
    with spring,
    transparent energy
   exchanged, engaged,
    sage leaf and sand cedar assimilate,
awakening, stretching
out each limb toward the light.
   Below the earth
   heavy apron'd women beneath the roots
   wide in the hips and thick-thighed,
   handsome women with heavy hair
   dip their buckets
   scoop water from the aquifer
   and haul it to the roots,
     that turn and twist up from the stiff earth
     like fairy tale roads leading to a green castle.
Green life drives through each blade of grass,
green life celebrates its renewal,
green life cares nothing about materialism,
   only chaotic beginnings,
   sapling Russian Olive trees that survived the winter
   patches of grass in the woods
     that hibernated beneath the fallen leaves, now rise
     armies of anonymous bushes and brush-trees
     along the Rio Grande, now rise,
ache,
create alliance, following the summoning of sunlight,
their fates,
their convictions fleshing out in green life, leaves, trees, grass,
  without dispute or analysis,
  their differences a thousand forms of gratitude,
  blend into thankfulness, a dialogue celebrating
    arrivals.

It's not about piles of cash,
military might or police states,
war or racism,
digital gadgets or global superpowers,
not criminally accusing the innocent
nor our national interest,
not privilege—
      but life cooperating
      life stored up in the leafless bough set free,
      life weaving its patterns during winter in the twig,
      life in the ditch waters flowing softly south,
      life laundering winter from its cores
            to accommodate
            the brimming fiesta of spring.

In each flower
is the journey of past pain,
in their beauty of how
to endure the pain and cope with the conflicts in life,
ease, stretch, crawl, unfold, fly and walk
to the other side of pain,
      where each fiber and breath and tissue is prompted to its highest
                                  expression,
      emerging to explore the light.

Our anger changes, transforms,
transfers, transmits dark, agonizing pain
into green life, green song, green hills,
      our hearts are seasonal journals of pain
      trying to learn the language
      that relieves our daily enforcement to tasks we hate,
      contributing to the green life along the river,
      that each day,
            expands my story and relates
            my own pains and sorrows.

This greening life tells my story
the broken snarling cottonwood logs
tell how I lived with anger and hurt, regretting
when I behaved badly.

The sage leaves' fragrance
makes such a big difference in my life,
feeling the blues for days,
a scent from the sage diffuses my sadness,
makes me feel safer
than all the security measures
        against terrorism.

Sometimes I stand on the river bank
and feel the water take my pain,
allow my nostalgic brooding
a reprieve.
The water flows south,
constantly redrafting its story
which is my story,
rising and lowering with glimmering meanings—
here nations drown their stupid babbling,
bragging senators are mere geese droppings in the mud,
radicals and conservatives are stands of island grass,
and the water flows on,
cleansing, baptizing Muslims, Jews and Christians alike.

I yearn to move past these days of hate and racism.

That is why this Rio Grande,
these trees and sage bushes
the geese, horses, dogs and river stones
        are so important to me—
        with them

I go on altering my reptilian self,
reaching higher notes of being
on my trombone heart,
pulsing out into the universe, my music
according to the leaf's music sheet,
working, with a vague indulgence toward a song
called
we the people.

19.

for Consuelo

And on this morning sweet Creator,
bless my children, bless me, take me into your waters
and let the spirits of the water
show me how to surmount my obstacles,
let the spirits of the water
give me their blessings.

> *Show me how to swirl*
> *around my obstacles with such grace.*
> *If dry islands and sandbars appears*
> *if I have dry periods of creativity,*
>> *if sometimes sadness appear*
>> *or hurt or pain and grief,*
>> *like the river's sandbars,*
>> *let tall river grass grow there, let*
>>> *Canada geese and mallards and cranes*
>>> *nest in my sadness.*

I'll tell you this—
I believe in the Spirits, in the eastern Night
that streams through my bellybutton
with an ancient woman who sews
existence with her golden thread
to all threads in the universe,
me to my ancestors, me to this earth
and I run with a golden thread trailing in my wake.

My prayer for you on this day is that
when you wake, golden threads may entangle your feet,
may golden threads tangle up your hands,
when you walk to a place that will harm you,
when you reach for something that will darken your heart,

let golden threads entangle you
and follow the thread back to your soul's purpose.

To the south, the Sacred Deer
vigilant, walks in the dark.
The darkness we must learn to love
as a mother's hand on a cold evening
as she leads us through streets we have never seen—
foreign pathways
will call us,
and that is good
but we must learn to trust our senses
our ears, our eyes
learn to let darkness mold, heal, reshape the way we listen,
teach us to walk lightly, to be wary when necessary,
then, let us walk in the forest at night
and sing our whispered love to the moon and trees.

To the south, our Ancestors
laugh at our mistakes. But they do not mock us,
they love us, are here with us, every step of the way.
I see them near,
and I pray to them, ask them to
Send this message of humble pleading
to my love, tell her the news of my love for her—
ancestors are good for carrying out love messages to my beloved.
So I stand facing south and call out my love for her.
I tell them: *you know me, I thank you humbly for caring for me,*
thank you for watching over me,
and I mean not to trouble you with my snifflings, whining wishes
but I am me, I must say I love her, I must say I want to be with her,
I must convey to you, ask you, please, carry this message of love
to the Creator that He may send it on to her.

I bow in honor of you my Ancestors. I bow,
and now offer these shelled pecan nuts for you.

Then the great Bear to the north—
May I ask you with open heart and open spirit
to accept my prayer this morning,
please bless me with your strength,
with your courage, your honesty, your eyes,
may you send me from your spirit to my spirit
a morsel of each, that I too may walk and breathe
with these gifts you offer me.

These prayers I offer to the world, to the sky and Mother Earth,
sky and earth, mother and father
who have always held me in their embrace and protected me,
always loved and listened and nourished me.

I am flower-nectar for the blue beak of day—
pierce my heart and suck from it the sweet honey.
I am a fish afraid of shadows and stirrings,
a fish whirling madly in the water of the Creator's music,
dancing in the water of the Creator's flowing,
in the Creator's rhythms, in the Creator's strumming of energy
in the Creator's love that shimmers every scale of me . . .

>Take me out of the Creator's water,
>I gag on the fishhooks of lies and betrayals,
>that leave me dying,
>gasping, my dead eyes
>blackberry jelly melting.

20.

I used to watch the old men
sitting deep in leather-cushioned arm chairs
next to a wood stove
in the pool hall,
paper open in their hands,
pipe or cigarette smoke clouding the air
filled with morning sunshine
leg flung over leg and their polished
shoes
lightly keeping beat to some internal nervous worry.
A fly would buzz around them,
land on their cotton cedar-smelling pants
or on their finger, the brim of their hats,
and after they'd had enough, they'd carefully
fold the paper, sit stock still until the fly
suspected nothing and they'd whack it,
a grin would crease their face
and they'd go back to reading again.
Then another fly would buzz around,
descend from the propeller blade fan above,
land on their knee or shirt cuff,
they'd eye it through old framed glasses,
and they'd repeat the same execution process . . .
For myself, I applaud the fly's bravery, its insistence
to barge in on our solemn moments
and remind us how insignificant we are;
just another sweeter smelling dung heap,
dying doing our dance as they, doing what
they were meant to do
makes them wiser than us who read all the papers in
the world
yet have forgotten to hear and celebrate the poet's song
echoing to us from all we've experienced.

21.

Two roadrunners in the field
    yesterday afternoon
    gray feathered, stiff twitching tails,
    sharp heads jerking alertly
        toward me as I pass them.
It's a warm afternoon,
dormant alfalfa fields recite poems
filled with nostalgic, but soothing memories.

    I pick up scores of beer cans
    scattered in the irrigation ditch,
        so many beer cans—
    quarts, six pack boxes and paper bags
    which I gather and mound up in a pile
    for the county jail crew along the highway to pick up.
The beer cans are symbols of my brother
and parents killed by alcohol,
and I repeat a prayer for those other brothers and sisters
drinking last night.

    We believe in the fairy tale of happiness
    as children
    then the jewels of our eyes shatter
    and sorrow tipped days
    pierce deep into our hearts.

The best love can offer is to be loyal
to the one we're with—
    I'm alone with my prayers,
    my breath, I jog along the irrigation ditch
    leaving half my life behind me
    fully prepared for my life ahead of me,

the air glowing with words
　　　we exchanged on the phone,
　　　word-stars in a galaxy
　　　I decipher designs that reveal
　　　our horoscopes of love as long and fulfilling.
You are not like others,
you are not a liar, you do not fester with jealousy
you do not make choices based on weakness
　　　you do not
　　　　　betray,
listen to others and act on their advice to win their approval,
you do not undermine this relationship from fear
you do not agitate, are not a dramatic queen
whose suppressed sexual urges have you one day a saint in church
and the next dog-styled over in porno heaven,
not spoiled, not wandering from bed to bed

no—
what I read in the words we share on the phone
that constellate us
with galaxies of happiness and sadness and fear and hope,
as we journey down the road
of our lives,
　　　and when we are hungry, we eat this meaning,
　　　when we are thirsty, we drink this purpose,
　　　when we are afraid, the meaning of us nourishes us
　　　when we are alone, the purpose of our journey accompanies us.

So the roadrunners said to me,
so infused with their own purpose,
and as I entered the forest path,
　　　a woodpecker tacka-tacka tacked above me
　　　its own prayers to the Creator
　　　on our behalf,

that we have a safe home for our child,
a strong home filled with humility and love,
a shelter for friends, a kitchen with food for all,
and on lazy afternoons, a bowl of ice-cream and nuts,
30's, 40's, 50's jazz songs
me writing a poem by the window overlooking the valley
you on the bed, nursing our son,
        your laughter a prayer to the wind . . .

22.

Black crows descend on the leafless cottonwood
along the bosque
bearing omens.
Even sad men
are given secrets to survive each day's loneliness.
The crows see me running along this path every other day
with a furious love in my heart
to clap, stamp and cry out
to the skies, the earth, the waters, the trees.

A month ago I was running along the beach in Venice,
dark, I couldn't see the ocean just hear
it gasping to breathe its passion,
as light at the horizon
birthed its first blossoming, and rose.

I wanted to wrench fish with my teeth from the sea and eat,
but in the dark, I ran,
I ran, like a widow's grieving wail, I ran, hoping for a sign
a trace, some evidence I could take with me
that would give me hope and as the light grew,
        snuggled in my black hooded sweatshirt
        my strong legs carrying me over the sand, leaping
        across inlet water channels,
           searching sand, foam, seaweed
           beach cluttered with useless broken shells,
I saw what looked like a large perfect seashell.

        I stopped, knelt down, after the ebb tide
        had slacked back,
        I reached for the sea shell,
surprised it was an infant's footprint—
           the infant's footprint better than a seashell.

And as light spread over the ocean, I saw an island
out in the ocean where hordes of seagulls gathered
                    clamoring at my treasure,
                        as if my discovery of a footprint
            was a gift from them,
            to step into the day
            as a child again stepping for the first time . . .

23.

When you entered my small apartment
      seemed the prayers I'd been mumbling for months
      bore fruit, I finally embraced you—
      but it's more than that,
you were good for my soul
I grew around you, I hatched out of my sadness,
flung the fragments of sorrow off,
      genuinely happy, absorbed in your kiss, your eyes,
      my heart felt so strong and alive and certain of itself
      I could have pounded in a hundred fence posts with my bare
                                            hand.

Hauling in your huge bags, going to exercise with you,
running in the river forest,
I was constantly aware of your presence
like a soft breeze coming through a prairie window
filled with wildflower and sweet grass fragrance.

      I felt comfortable with you
      as if you were what I had been wanting to learn
      for a long time,
      the way a child learns to walk forward,
      and when you came I quit stumbling and falling down
                 and you felt good.
No whining or moaning or morose mood swings,
no suspicions, no fears looming over you,
you accepted me, swung your arms wide beckoning me forth,
held this wild jaguar man I am
      and allowed me to curl up in your lap
in your arms over your legs
      and trust you, love you, finally.

24.

I've traveled always with a memory of you,
each day is the page of a family photo album,
where I sat in a café gently caressing your picture.
My knees I use to kneel on to pray,
my lungs I use to breathe in breath out,
my hands I use to feel things in this world,
                            still search you out.

I remember we climbed Mount St. Francis peak
an all day hike to the peak
where you became the crystalline air
that chilled my flesh comfortably with the knowledge I was living
my life hard, healthy, purposefully, and spiritually.

But mostly, the memory I carry of you
is that of a wound,
as if I were a soldier, I unwrap the bandages, clean the wound,
wrap it again with soft white gauze because each day
without you is a war I survived.

I cannot sleep on my left side because it is where I turned
when you slept next to me but you are not there now.
I cannot cook out of certain pans because you cooked with them,
and so it goes, my whole existence is permeated with your presence,
and whatever I do, we've done together at one time.

25.

It is not so easy to speak of love
so I'll speak of other things, that might,
ever so slightly reveal a subtle side of love,
like the way a dry desert wind will blow a woman's face veil
revealing her beautiful mouth—
> wearing a veil then, that moment when the woman's eyes
> catch you in their sights,
> the list of errands jotted down to do
> suddenly mean nothing—
in that moment you are ready to leave your home,
go with the money in your pocket
as long as her heart is with yours,
you make no plans,
> you just follow the wind.

When I run in the morning, I look for plants
that will speak to me
offer some sign I can translate into
instructions on how to live
> in the same manner a cellist is a brown flower
> and grows when it is watered by dark rains of sorrow.
> When running in the morning,
> I sometimes try to talk myself out of growing,
> why live, when mistakes keep happening,
> why breathe, if you can't breathe with dignity,
> why love, if you can't love all the time?
You see, I am a high-wire walker,
who picks the windiest days of the year to walk the wire.

I believe the Creator brought us together,
and I respond by naming all the flowers I see
> Stacy   Stacy   Stacy.

I holler my prayers to the two red-tailed hawks
circling for prey by the river, above the cottonwoods,
asking them to carry my earnest wishes to God,
for God to ponder . . .
                    then I feel the pain in my legs,
                    breathe deep to resume my jog,
                    and for an instant, believe
                    God has heard me. . . .

If I repeat your name enough times it becomes a mantra
that centers me in my flesh,
your life, how you live, your beauty, your breasts
ass and legs, laughter and hair and eyes
I see in the violin player
when suddenly a fiery awareness overtakes her,
          when she shivers,
her bow draws forth like bolts of lightning
saying your name,
and when she flings her head down and up, begging the music to reach
what she yearns for,
                    with all of this,
                    if you asked me to spell the word heart
                    I would not as other do in diamonds or poems
                    but in the sand, and I would spell it *p a i n*
                    and know that by morning, the tide
                         would have washed it away.

Were I to look inside your heart,
I would see the tide, Stacy. . . the tide . . .

26.

If I can go through today
mindful of the significance
of the black-winged butterfly I saw yesterday by the ditch bank,
first to appear this year
to understand its black wings fluttering a kind of aerial graffiti
urging my heart to dance about the air
celebrating even sorrow,
because the day is beautiful
because I breathe and weep
because I feel lonely;
to understand the flighty language of this black butterfly
and think of my Chicano aunt as black as this butterfly
and the way she sang in the morning
her tribal healing joy to the world
when she stirred the steaming oatmeal
entranced by sound,
that drove deep down in Mother Earth's black dance-mud body—
enchanting me with her deep drum voice
that made the linoleum of our house
hardened hut dirt
and me a rooted man with a heart made of braided roots.

I feel my lips extend out; my hands become sea waves,
my knotted hair full of feathers.
I let my head loll forward and dance
this moment
in a wild-howling leap-skip dance
mimicking the black butterfly
in my holy, Chicano-defiant way to communicate to you
my love of people, my love of water, my love of dirt,
my love of distances that tell me their secrets of loneliness;
how white moon is full this morning

at dawn how I woke and saw her yawning erotically
on the horizon at dawn,
how I wished I had your warm body next to mine
to pull and stretch and dip my hands into you,
reach up into your heart
the way a Chicano loses his hands in leaves
when picking chili,
reach my hands into you woman the way bells plunge their sound
into silence
and shake in your thick-lipped mouth and bone joints,
the way white moon hung there on the horizon
so you know my way, so you know my habits, so you know my

customs

and know me as your man
smelling of you, fragrant with your skin smell
your hair scents, your vaginal and anal smells—
let them be on me the way a barn smells
of dung and hay and cows and milk,
let you be in me and me in you
the way the black butterfly fully lives its flight
is how

        woman, this heart of mine beats
        dum-doom dum-doom dum-doom
        and hear me, this man, that sings
        like the black butterfly on the light air, scattering its message.

Yet, you would take this song
and crush it in your hands
you would take this song
and bite it with your teeth
you would take this song
and drown my words
because you do not understand my language.
How I speak is how grass slowly greens

how I speak is how the hawk
showed its red tail to me,
how I speak is how I hold you sometimes
holding you in my arms
is a tribal yell that goes
holen-my-omen
holen-my-omen,
and the hawk taught me to shhsss
and the butterfly taught me design
and between the shhhsss and design
I create this ho-ma-omen song
I sing my holen-my-omen
I chant my holen-my-omen song
to you, to celebrate your smile, your laughter, your tears,
look around!

These are beautiful days of creating ourselves,
look around!
These are days of searching for ourselves
in flights of our winged family,
look around!
Hold your man, hold your man,
that's what the white full moon sang softly to you
this morning
while I rode in the streets off to gather more poems
for the day,
the moon howled hold your woman
and each blade of grass, tree limb, the very gray and black color
of dawn
bellowed me a language that sent me
walking along the Rio Grande
repeating this love the river gives me
these prayers she offers me
this fire that it is,

I carry in me, fire-me, fire-me, fire-me
and now I dance as a flame might dance, I speak as a flame
might speak, I touch as flame might touch, I yearn as a flame yearns—
and yet,
you bring water to douse me
your bring wet wood to warm us
you wear fire-retardant clothing
you do not sing to the light that flames give
you moan from the burn
you do not hum the heat up from your loins
you let the drum grow gray with morning ice
and the skin crack from neglect.

I rub a dream of mine each morning
before I blow on it,
before I ask it questions I wrap it in deer hide,
I throw dirt over it
I ask it to remember the pain
I tell it to be humble,
I instruct it to be like the mallard ducks
I saw yesterday,
first one going north, then its mate
quickly following its male
and I thought how they mate forever
and I told my dream
you must learn that lesson well, dear dream
go into this day
smelling of dirt and working hands and smoke and sage
and lose yourself in these green sage days
lose your black butterfly heart in this day
on a wild flight
and when strangers ask of your map and direction
tell the people you are following your joy.

These days I unexpectedly run into people
unfamiliar to me, yet claim we met years ago
during college days—
one-night lovers from the past
met at a poetry reading in a blues bar,
or an academic seminar—
when they declared
themselves poets of the people, advocates of the poor,
but since have become rich humanware
in expensive homes, dining
with high-society neighbors,
        and their once rude and youthful rebellion
        debased as a polite trinket of conversation.

But I vaguely recall one-night encounters,
and how I later rejected their offers
for a steady relationship—
now so many years later
these rejected lovers
bitter about abandoning their dream
accuse me of being a provocateur,
pile my table with platters of their rage
play with words as if words had no spirit,
leave their complaints at my door
like overdue bills,
their anger disguised in a mask of friendly concern
they insult my small life
they remind me of my failures
they lavish over my mistakes
they excavate my past
they will not let me forget
the wasteland, my indulgence, my thirst for destruction,
they want to satisfy themselves on broken guitars
torn cello strings, and lovers
who wear a key around their neck.

Show them your sadness and they will mock you
show them your compassion and they will be cynical
sing them your songs and they will not hear them
offer up your heart and they will try to change it
give all of your self as you are
and they will not accept you—
and after you have spent your day seeing them as they are
they will say you cannot see them,
after you have flattered them how they are superior
sinless, human beings,
they will say you have robbed their enthusiasm for life
that your truth has deprived them of their innocence
that you do not receive them as they are
that your promises are no good
that your words are as false as a married man's steps
scuttling away from his secretary's office,
and they will tell you that your passions are hammers pounding them
                                                                          down
the things you believe are mere fantasies to enrapture hearts
that you no longer dream of life as life can offer itself to you
in its splendor and magnificence,
that your needs are selfish,
your emotions whimsical, your honesty based on a lie
that you foster with each breath,
and after all of this was leveled at me
I put my jacket on and walked to the Rio Grande banks
seeking counsel from the waters, an ancestor to appear in the air,
beneath the prayer tree I stand under and pray each day.

I want answers
to rise from the ground
like Christ on Easter Sunday,
to remove the stone from my heart,
that I might rise from my own death,

a better man,
and sing the black butterfly's metamorphosis
as it changes and ascends toward its ultimate cosmic costume
resting on the twig or leaf a moment
then sacrificing itself to the wind
and by day's end laying dead in dust
contented, fulfilled.

27.

Were there a way to say thank you
for the friendship I have
                              received
in this life,
I would say it but
words are like uncooked pinto beans
without flavor, without juice, without sauce and chili.
           I want to feed the spirits of my words
and yearn sometimes that my gratitude
were a cluster of trees at the edge of the field
I greet happily each day on my walk.

               Since some thief stole my dog Teddyboy,
               (a leopard-spotted Catahoula),
               I have kept my sadness to myself.
Only with the trees and fields can I share my sorrow these days,
only with the field do I holler out sometimes
asking the trees and fields to return my love for life,
my enthusiasm for living,
praying sometimes before the river
           that as I breathe its air—
           air-creator river,
how clouds form, rain becomes, river is,
then water steams up, becomes air again,
and as my friends breathe the air I breathe
I ask that as they inhale breath to live
they also inhale an awareness of my love for them,
that as they step each day for their coffee, their clothes, their
                                                       bathrooms
I become the field in their soul they can share their sadness with,
their love with, their innermost secrets with,
because I do not want all that I was given in life

from my heart and soul
to be meaningless or lost on trivial whims.
I don't want them to think or feel
that our love was just pleasure.
I want myself in their lives even if I am far away
as this field I pass each day
is in my life;
every day it offers me some new insight into my own struggle,
every day it gives me soothing calm and teaches me patience,
every day light plays in it in a different way
shadows reveal other secrets in it,
so in lovers' minds, I want my love
to be seen in various ways:
that behind the hurt they first saw
is a passionate love,
behind the betrayal they first accused me of
now is a serene insight that makes them walk stronger,
that makes them look south, to where I live
in a small little room and love me,
as I adore this small, insignificant field
that over the past year and a half has grown to mean all the riches
in life.
Its slow, mesmerizing music sinks and swells my bones with sweetness
and I must cry out when passing it,
I love you!
The field hawk stares at me
inspecting an awkward fellow,
the squirrel speed-shuffles through the crispy underbrush,
the woodpecker with its orange/red-black plumage
above in the looming branches—swats
air briskly, crackling airy light
showering me with an idea for a gift.

On my walks in the bosque
I have collected woodpecker feathers

and have enough to make a feather fan for a friend.
Since she has told me she cannot settle down,
and has told me she is an orphan too,
this fan will be a power talisman
to help her find a place to settle in
as the woodpecker makes its home in hard wood,
let it give her power to chisel herself out a home
some place, some city, some day.

Do not waste time with the fearful
bimbos clacking cheetah teeth
for whimsical pleasures—
    love from deep in the heart-wells
    where ancient sands glimmer up through the water—
        pray to the woodpecker
        to help us make a home
        in the hard wood of our words,
        pray to the woodpecker
        to bless us
        making our actions, behavior and gestures,
        entrances for people seeking refuge from the rain.

28.

I am a precarious fellow, on edge
wandering like the river, the way it
                sniffs out banks,
                floods over into paths,
                making hikers slip,
                laying low in the shallows,
                or asleep with dreams full of smug mud-carp.
I round a hedge-sage wall of dense brush
and spreading out before me unexpectedly I see a bend in the river,
                it stuns me
                that one day I may be as sincere with myself,
                through the changes of being a human being,
                turn to see myself
                flowingly, gracefully as the river.

29.

Running in the bosque, it's all about relations
to the trees, birds, fields, the ground I run on,
my much abused heart—
        it's no news to anyone
        who's truly lived
how much we abuse our hearts
fouling them up with cocaine nights
tequila shots
    and cheap fucks,
        we've all had that long car drive
        leaving a city
        by ourselves or with a lover
        cigar box filled with drugs
        thinking we were starting our life over,
that around the next curve our fate awaited us
when we could live the life we're meant to live
with a companion who would never lie, never betray,
never go out on us,
        a job that allowed us to dance, write poetry, meet
        interesting people working on their lives—
but false starts abounded in my life
and the cottonwood trees tell the story
of the life I always wanted,
        being true to themselves,
always there for the hawk, the crows,
offering their branches with unquestioning compassion.

I have gone to the river to grieve before these trees,
as if they were great gray mothers who had marched
through snow, cloaked in leaves,
bare skinned without leaves, enduring the freezing rain,
who carried me in their arms, close to their breast.

I've heard them mourning on windy nights,
    groaning their loneliness
    like teeth gnashing in a fevered patient's mouth
    from haunting nightmares assaulting her.
These trees do their dance, do their lives, do their miracles
on me,
and their acceptance of me has been so complete
    these grayed haired women dance around me,
    these golden haired women sing my heart alive,
    these molting haired women cry up to the moon my meaning,
    these green haired women shake and wildly slap the air
and in their silence, in their brooding moods
tell me to weep—
    Learn to weep,
    learn to hold yourself sweet child, sweet boy
    learn to wrap your arms around yourself sweet child,
roamer, wild wanderer, come rest on our legs,
come rest against our breast and weep young man—
    O gypsy child,
    outlaw in the night,
    you wanted to rage against the world and make it right
    know we women of the forest love you,
    serve you our souls in the form of leaves
that when you run on the path between us
    we sweep up your suffering,
    we soften the path for your feet
    we whisper you to believe
        believe in yourself
and weep out your hurt, weep out your confusion
    weep your love for your self
    because here, on this path
you tried to outrun your pain after losing love
outrun your addictions
    outrun your fears
        outrun your confusion

and we have always been here, soothing your solitary wandering,
awaiting you each day
    offering you our spiritual blessings
    to go on sweet night-wanderer,
    teaching you how to open your heart again
    as a newborn infant opens its mouth taking its first breath of air
    we give birth to you,
        women of the forest,
        infuse your veins with our blood,
        sucked from the center of Mother Earth,
        earth-juice in our roots that fattens our waistlines
        extends our branches, lengthens our looming heights,
this is our blessing, each leaf holds Mother root juice
and when you pass below, a figure running all your life from life,
it is then that our leaves like a million hands turn in the wind
and shower you with blessings, filtering through your nose, your mouth,
to lessen the weight of your iron heavy life,
to ease you, take part of your heart in our arms and rock you, sweet man,
                             rock you

in our leaf-lullabies, let you know you are loved,
    as we teach of loving yourself.

30.

So I dreamed my life would be what it is today
there was no choice-
> I run, rhythmically breathing,
>> honoring muscle, bone, hair, tooth,
>> my heart a pheasant that explodes from the bush
>> and vanishes into the brush.

I have come here a thousand times and each time is new,
familiar yet strange, to see myself
tracked by the bosque,
> hear myself questioned by the water,
gazed upon by the hawk
> whose glare questions my sincerity,
> and I pray hard for people I love,
> pray that my lovely woman comes to me,
and when I turn, I suddenly see her running beside me again
see her quietly within reach of me
hear her saying she will never leave,
she will be at my side
will work out the changes,
will devour my love as I hers,
will believe in me, forgive me, lead me, wrap her heart
around mine like a sailor's knot in the rope that holds the sail
taut and steady against any stormy wind.
> I run
> like a stream flowing through woods,
> thanking all of Creation, in deep gratitude
>> to the Creator for being alive this moment,
>> to appear with all my faults
>> on this ditch bank, along the riverbank,
>> exhausted, weary, struggling to keep a steady pace
because I know there is really no distance, that time does not really

exist

there is only now, the step
that lifts but never lands, never sets itself down
but always, keeps itself flying because we fly
I know we do, that this skin
> and bone and limbs merely go through the gestures
> of eating an orange when I return home,
> pick up a pot to cook breakfast,
> open the refrigerator to make a sandwich
while I do this,
I know that somewhere else, I am flying,
I am in the heart of a woman who loves me,
> and there, in her heart,
> I am a wolf,
> a big snowy furred wolf with red eyes
> cantering through a forest high along on a ridge of her heart.
> I stop to howl when I hear her,
> I howl answering her howl,
> > and I keep loping on in her heart to a place beneath a tree
> > where I curl up and sleep through the night.

31.

To step out at 5:30 into the sparkling dark
feel my skin animal again,
be present for my own appearance,
gathering myself slowly over the days and nights
months and days, ghosts of my dream to be
like fog around seaport lamps on the dock.

I walk, looking out to sea,
    in my black navy coat, collar turned up,
    my beanie cap on,
    jeans and T-shirt,
      I haven't cared much about the values
      of this world.
        I spit out to sea.

To step out into the night
have my voice spread out as a winter snow, my words gleaming frost
on everything, and in the field, faraway, a lone man
walks toward me—
      a man who rises early to walk in the dark dawn
      think deeply that one day he'll become dust
and can't overcome the contradictions
that come with being human—
      how it is possible that we're capable of dreaming
      such love into existence,
when ultimately the grand display of all our romance
    simmers ignominiously in the ash pit of our betrayals?

I am one of those men who rise at dawn.
I don't talk, I'm learning to seek silence
    in myself
      to accept the violations I've committed,

and doing so, sometimes the sun is a black sun
sometimes there is no hope to continue
sometimes I wonder what my hands are good for—
      and then I find myself in a woman's kitchen
      and her child leaps up on the chair
      and wants to bake cookies with me—
      my love for life and people returns that instant,
and I want to re-promise myself all my promises again,
recount all my virtues,
go knocking on every door down the street
rousing people to step out and dance in the street again—
    come, bring your incense, candles, songs,
        I want us to bury our heads in each other's breasts
        with joy, and in the dance
    release our sorrows to the air, scatter them off
    our heels, shatter them in our clapping.

I'm tired of the world finding fault
in those who don't abide by their ridiculous standards,
tired of those pie-cheek counselors,
    tv-therapy sessions, and celebrity advice
      and I want to be
      an ordinary dog
      in any front yard
      squatting on the grass
      taking a shit.

32.

Wintry, brown-gray leaves carpet the forest path.
These are like my impulses
      sunlight gleams from,
in a hurry to leap from the branch they were born from,
they tear away to adventure out
      and die, sink into earth,
      become granulated beings diffused into mineral worlds.

      On these paths I have hugged women I've loved,
      looked in to their eyes as into their promises
      filled with innocent wonderment
      forgotten weeks later on a beach or in the mountains,
      where they've shared their hearts with others,
      the promised parts they spoke as only mine,
      became game-feasts for the hunters,
      they drank and stumbled in other arms
      sucked and opened themselves
          and in the morning, when they called,
          their voices no longer impassioned,
          but lazy with last night's liquor,
             and numb with betrayal . . .

Leaves have taught me to beware,
be cautious they say, as I study where a caterpillar ate their edge,
be discriminating they say, as I notice how one died early
on a twig snapped from its branch—
      each time I fall in love,
      I hold a green leaf in my palm,
      let it whisper to me its desires,
      study its newness, its gloss, its green life.

I wonder when it will be underfoot as I run,
when will I step on it, at what moment
will it release its hold on its origins, and leave, happily
dancing through the air, for a moment ecstatic,
indulging in flight,
then ever slowly, descend, descend, descend,
      and then know the death of love
      as particle by particle
      it diffuses on the air, is gorged on by other creatures
      as soil buries it, wind ravishes it, sun blisters it,
      as my dog and me pass lightly by, sniffing, stepping,
running over them once so brave and strong and pure and innocent,
inhaling their dusty death into my own lungs.
      I thank them for surrendering,
      for dying
      giving only a frail stir of defiance,
      a crisp crackling in the brush
            where, among insects and lizards,
            the dust of leaves birth green
            shoots of young
            that perhaps my grandchildren will jog under
            when I too have reached for my dream wholly
                        and fully,
            when I am gone,
            when my death gives birth to a tree
            and I will then be a leaf
            loving a greater love than I have now,
            the love of a bright sunny morning on my face?

33.

The sun finally comes up,
I put on a Dylan CD, *Live at Telluride*.
> His moan-drone, up-tempo nasal voice
> his heel-kicking guitar beat
> and the sun spreading evenly over all of life is good.

I light sage, bless my house, say my prayers,
think of the way pigeons swoop and sway
over the apartment tops,
how someone this morning
thanks God for not waking up drunk,
others for not betraying their love,
others for keeping their love intact with words, with sincerity,
and driving to the post office, picking up my mail,
then on the phone with my cousin
laughing at our jokes until we couldn't laugh any more
> over to the coffee shop to pick up
> my latte with soy milk and two brown sugars,

and while my corn meal coagulates on the stove
and my garlic head is roasting,
I compose this poem, to my friend,
celebrating the small things—garlic, oatmeal, coffee,
soy, music, sage, prayers, friendship, laughter,
> setting off on this day
> prepared to honor the flame in each of us.

34.

I forget to pray, feel sluggish and mean,
until I think of the river, how it flows, at this hour
its silvery sheen is darkened by night sky,
stars over the black surface
   white necklace beads my lover
   flung into the water
   vowing never to forget my love—
   to be strong enough
   to be betrayed again, the river attaches itself,
   unattaches itself:
   a lesson that to love entails an agreement
   to be hurt again.

I agree as I breathe in the chill air,
agree as I turn from the bank and slowly walk
into the forest;
   notice how some tree trunks are twisted,
   how some grow sideways, others cracked,
others growing wildly like the mane of a lion,
and others shyly slipping unnoticeably into small spaces
their sapling branches gracefully expressing their timidity.
Sex, fevered panting love, thigh opening lust moans
and wet volcanic explosion
the trembling that merges us
in complete surrender
   to another soul and body,
   is what these trees do their dance for,
   is why those mountains to the east keep moving their
              shadows and
   sunlight in and out of hollows and canyons,
is what defines the core of my words to you
   each have the rings of a hundred year old tree,
   my words are old, but the center of each word

has a moist brown beginning spot where it was born,
uttered out, called out, celebrating
my meeting you.

Celebrating how the tree seed took root on my tongue
and you see
in my mouth a forest, crows flying out
from mouth, red-tailed hawks, geese, herons
scattering out from my words to you
migrating to your hands
to your hips, your vagina,
your legs—
your laughter a black coffee a short brown woman
in El Salvador has just made and its aroma permeates
the whole house, your dark brown laughter
drifts out of the roads and its black scents
excite the monkey, stray dogs yap,
young women sniffing it in the air
and get wet remembering their young man's lips
kissing their nipples . . .

Yes, this morning I think of the river,
how kind it has been to me
like an old singer I go to each day to listen to,
it fills the clay cup of my heart up with its whispering fables,
easing my loneliness—
and all around me
this crazy labyrinth of boughs going in every direction
is an adventure of the heart I know well,
and answer for me
why some men don't return home,
why others changed,
why some died early
and others still electrify the dusk quietness
with their verve and boundless love of creative life.

35.

to Dave and Amy

You ever have one of those days
so intense with your developing dream
rising out of earth, from the horizon,
becoming real, one of those days
filled with conversations with friends
so nurturing and honest, where you discuss
with a kind of wonder, the pain you've overcome,
and heartbreaks you've suffered, and hurt through,
              yet endured,
to move on, into a day like this
loving stronger, happiness more grounded and deeper,
embedded in your bones a newly discovered mineral
that has cured you of your uncertainties,
crystallized your healing process into a routine dream
you live now,
        breathe in and out now, touch, engage, act upon,
        amend as you change and correct yourselves
            to live more days like this?

I drive to Abiqui, meet Dave building my cabin there,
stretch out the plans on the hood of my truck,
pointing my finger along the blue lines,
saying, "Add a larger loft, and here a basement with sleeping
                                accommodations
for friends that might drop in unexpectedly."
        Then they leave back to Durango.

        Driving the muddy, snow-crusted dirt road out
snugged in my blue checkered Scottish Carmichael scarf, light cotton
                                 jacket,
brown Telluride beanie cap and leather climbing boots,
        feeling good after paying the workers,

I'm tire-sloshing oozing red canyon clay
toward home,
when I meet
Elude walking with his two sons down the road,
and I hand him a check, yelling, "I'll talk to you later."
I race to catch Dave
who drove off with the workers,
slam the gas pedal down, bucking mud off cleat tires around mountain
                                                                curves
and catch them, just as they're leaving the canyon,
telling Amy to jump in, I'm taking her to Durango.

One of those days
when we reach the old wood, brass and red brick Stratter
                                                            Hotel
and they only have two rooms left, one
for my homies Efren and Valentin,
and one for me and her.

I wake to snow after months of drought—
snowed good, two feet horse-inching snow,
snowed good as a harp-playing frenzied scraggly harp player
blowing mean back-dues of pain down down down
on the streets so white so pure so right
        he closes the road, makes all the people
snuggle up in a smoky bar and sit and listen to him play,
his cloud heavy brooding tunes
snow snow snow blues,
questing wrenching spunk-blues
that make even a dead dog rise up and dance-bark
chasing after his chrome-bumpered harp-blowing notes
barreling down in a sixteen-wheeler mack-force roar
into the heart's lonely highway.

Yeah, one of those days,
when I felt so content and good inside,
I finally settled down and let Valentin drive
while I cuddled up in the back with my lap-top on my knees
and started writing, almost running out of gas and stopping
at this old, rusting one-pump roadside Indian cafe
where I walked in, bundled all up but wearing gym shorts,
made those old Navajos in their bow-legged worn jeans and scruff
                                              cowboy hats
laugh at me and I laughed with them at myself,
Chicano Buddha in a blizzard wearing shorts;
    that kind of day I had,
    when it felt my two friends and me had been together for years,
    when a day lasted a year,
    and friendships
    pulverized all the black stones of worry in my soul.

36.

This morning, I chant my prayers running along the river—
I am not sure if my prayers
spring from the dormant frost chilled fields
or if they come from the river's water,
  its silvery strings plucked
  by weed islands it goes around, dancing like a woman
  around the island all full of shine and happiness,
  kicking up its black heels made of broken tree branches—

but closer to the bank the river's easy current becomes
a storyteller's voice, playing its fiddle, the easy country voice
tells me how I've pleased some, upset others,
  yet how I have, putting one step in front of the other,
  come here every day,
  to sit on the bank like an old cowboy
    chewing a grass strand in my mouth,
    holding a few pebbles in my hand,
    watching the river go by.

And beyond, to the east,
I pray to the Sandia Mountains to lend their strength,
give me their grace of power—how
subtly the canyons reveal themselves on some days,
other days they look blue, change to green, shrink, magnify up,
and inside me an old man sits in the shadows
rises with his guitar and strums it,
strums it fast, hard, and in my blood a dreamer stands and signs
how life is worth nothing without the inner love,
the inner fever, the inner madness we call God, we call Creator
    and the poet in me claps, yeah! Claps, sways hips, moves feet
to the yeahing and clapping in my blood!

Opening my mouth, I pray
Great Creator bless me with your strength,
as I move now, as I dance now,
as I shake my hands and hips and head and shoulder
and I yell yeah! yeah! yeah! yeah!

I feel to the south the Deer
offer me its blessings, to the west
my Ancestors offer me their love,
to the north the Bear
offers me its courage and patience,

     and again
on this ground, this dirt, under these trees, on this path
beneath the cottonwoods I have walked under for a year,
I am a new born bleating lamb
running all over the field looking for its mother,
for the milk I suckled to dance away my sorrow,
dancing away my doubts, dancing away my troubles
came from those old hands and those old instruments of river and
                                     wood,
not from money, not from being right.

We were all wrong, we all had troubles, we all had pains
and we all gasped for breath and danced,
     and even a quiet man, a peaceful man,
a man walking this labyrinth each day searching his heart for wisdom
to live by and thank the universe for its blessings
can dance, dance in his prayers.

37.

When my heart was broken
I conferred with colleagues of cottonwoods,
when I wanted to go into the streets at night
and curse out of every credit-card carrying fool,
ring in the New Year with rage of the imprisoned, of the
                                        addicts and drunks,
take it down to the racists' doorsteps
and make them choke on their own blood
as I beat them down like tent stakes in the ground,
then I sought advice from the mallards,
not a clue to connect them to the humanity
ski-resort bunnies, who get their kicks
from hotel porno flicks, chanting yoga mantras,
and all that money, security, and what
                                        others think,
and when I desperately needed to scream, to get away
                                        from this world
to alleviate my sadness
sorrow, depression and loneliness,
I don't flush through pages of the bible
but go to the river's edge to hear God's voice,
pray, ask forgiveness for my stupid ways,
reading Thomas Merton poems,
I turn to the four directions
and ask the powers,
the sacred energies,
the fierce forces that have created me
humble me: *Please allow a wisp of light*
have mercy on this man who stumbles so easily,
erases all the good he's done
who sometimes could care less,
who always is blinded by so much beauty here,
who thanks the Creator for the gift of life, of breath

of love, of friends, of work, of struggle—
and then suddenly,
      as I am walking down the forest trail,
      just above me a V of Canada geese flies north,
      three sets of mallards fly out of the mother ditch,
      horses gallop in the fields,
          a squirrel clings to the bark of a tree watching me,
          a woodpecker hammers his beak in the tree high above,
and surrounded in thick forests, I cannot see the river
but hear on its banks hundreds of birds
chattering away, and then they rise
like a king's entrance on the balcony to the public
to give his speech to the hordes below,
      they pass overhead,
      and I stop, listen, praise them, obey them.

38.

I'm having these strange, wild dreams.
       There was a time when the future
       could blow away like so many garlic skins
       and I wouldn't have noticed
but now,
thinking of the future, in dreams I see myself
as the young vaquero, a boy with a cowboy hat
       rawhide vest, chaps and boots
       two guns in my holster.
"Leave him alone," the voice in my dreams says.
"The boy holds no answers to the future."

Then a dream-voice advises me
to let go of the ones I love,
burn the plans for building my own prairie house,
quit figuring how much money I'm going to make
if all my schemes unfold perfectly,
quit reaching desperately for things or people
that I foolishly believe will stop time,
       and freeze the present.

Go into any city and ask anyone
for directions into the future and they will offer you
their Gods, their drugs, their women.
For a moment you will keep pace with this illusion.

But then a day like this one arrives,
gray landscape cast over with your nostalgia,
when you realize even priests and convicts have things in common,
both are on a mission,
both are building their houses of stone
so when they are away and there is a forest fire

it won't burn as quickly as a log cabin—
while common people aspire to have relationships
made of charred remains of paradise.

Be that as it may,
when those exquisite moments
to indulge myself in lies
to cool the embering in my soul
arrive at my door, smiling and friendly,
tempt me with pleasures
that for a second
blind me to myself
allow me to forget my journey
and for a moment obscure my destination,
I then must engage the moment with the certainty
of a blade,
act in the fullness of me
with the greenness of an avocado,
must turn all sides of myself to the sun
and still know as the tomato
that here there will be green spots
the sun didn't catch.

My beliefs imbue me
as the carrot's orange imbues it,
as lettuce over-leafs itself in becoming a head of lettuce.

I go walking this morning
seeking roses in the snow,
see how the snow hides in the forest
see how my dreams hide in the future—

I love you,
is what I feel when I look at the mountains,

my blue mountains
gather fog and snow drifts
the way a man throws a horse blanket over the back
of his horse, slaps the saddle on it,
with a muscled grip, snugs the cinch up,
then rides off,

        is how I love you.

39.

Yesterday, the sunshine made the air glow
pushing me like a sixteen-year-old
to toss my shirt off, and run along the river shore,
splashing in the water, wading out to the reeds,
my heart an ancient Yaki drum
and I believed,

      more than believed,

      the air beneath trees was female blue dancers

      I approached, and there in the dry leaves, in the crisp twigs,

      I turned softly as if dancing with a blue woman made of air,

                                      sunlight,

          in shrub-weed skirts.

          I knew the dance that would please the Gods,

          I knew the dance that would make the river water

          smile glistening ever silvering,

          I knew the dance steps that praised my ancestors.

Yeah, I wanted to write you a poem woman
for two days,
and today it was gray and snowy and overcast,

      about how I startled the mallards from their shallow
refuge beneath the Russian olive trees
and how the male purposely

          came close to me

          diverting my attention to it

      its female love went the other way

      risking its life,

      that's what I saw,
the male fly before the hunter's rifles, circle in sights of hunters
and take the shots, the roaring rifle blast

                    after blast
and circle beyond over the fields to meet its female companion.

That's how I miss you, that's how I wanted to write you a poem
since we left
        you one way
        me another way. I was the male
        taking with me the hunters that would harm you
        risking my heart so yours wouldn't be hurt,
        fronting myself as possible prey
        so you could escape,
        that kind of poem
                I am writing you now.

Circling as hunters aim down on me
while you rise, rise, rise into the blue sky
        and meet me over in the next fields.

        I wanted to write you a poem for two days now
            to tell you how happy I was,
            seeing a white crane arc
                between banks in the irrigation ditch
                with furious effort, its big wings flapping
                    like an awkward nine-year-old kid
                    much taller than others his age
                    with size twelve sneakers
                    flapping down the basketball court.

But once the white crane
found its balance, its wings their grace, it glided more perfectly
than a ballet dancer's leap across air,
            all of its feathers ballet dancer's toes,
            all of its feathers delicate dancers
            all of its feathers, in motion
                made me believe in myself,
but more,
            when it rose, swooped up,
            the line of ascent up

made me think of the curve of your spine,
how I traced my finger down your spine
when you slept,
your spine,
is the ascent of the crane
toward the sunshine,
and my hands my face my torso and chest and legs and hips
became air, a blue cold artic air
you glided up in your song of winter love.

Contemporary American Poetry
from New Directions

John Allman

Curve Away from Stillness

Loew's Triboro

Jimmy Santiago Baca

Black Mesa Poems

Immigrants In Our Own Land & Selected Early Poems

Martín & Meditation on the South Valley

Winter Poems Along the Rio Grande

Kamau Brathwaite

Ancestors

Black + Blues

MiddlePassages

Anne Carson

Glass, Irony and God

Hayden Carruth

Asphalt Georgics

For You

From Snow and Rock, from Chaos

Tell Me Again How the White Heron Rises and
Flies Across the Nacreous River at Twilight
Toward the Distant Islands

Cid Corman

Livingdying

Nothing / Doing: Selected Poems

Sun Rock Man

Robert Creeley

Echoes

If I Were Writing This

Just in Time: Poems 1984–1994

Life & Death

So There: Poems 1976–1983

Windows

Lawrence Ferlinghetti

A Coney Island of the Mind

A Far Rockaway of the Heart

Americus, Book I

How to Paint Sunlight

These Are My Rivers: New & Selected Poems 1955–1993

Wild Dreams of a New Beginning

Thalia Field

Point and Line

Forrest Gander

Science & Steepleflower

Torn Awake

Allen Grossman

The Ether Dome and Other Poems New and Selected

How to Do Things With Tears

Sweet Youth: Poems by a Young Man and an Old Man

Paul Hoover

The Novel

Susan Howe

The Europe of Trusts

Frame Structures: Early Poems 1974–1979

The Midnight

The Nonconformist's Memorial

Pierce-Arrow

Mary Karr

The Devil's Tour

Viper Rum

Bernadette Mayer

A Bernadette Mayer Reader

Midwinter Day

Michael McClure

Rain Mirror

Rebel Lions

Simple Eyes

Toby Olson

    Human Nature

    We Are the Fire

Michael Palmer

    At Passages

    Codes Appearing: Poems 1979–1988

    The Lion Bridge: Selected Poems 1972–1995

    The Promises of Glass

Jerome Rothenberg

    A Book of Witness: Spells & Gris-Gris

    New Selected Poems 1970–1985

    A Paradise of Poets

    Vienna Blood

Peter Dale Scott

    Coming to Jakarta

    Crossing Borders

    Listening to the Candle

    Minding the Darkness

Gary Snyder

    The Back Country

    Look Out

    Myths & Texts

    Regarding Wave

    Turtle Island

Rosmarie Waldrop

A Key Into the Language of America

Blindsight

Reluctant Gravities

Please visit our website

www.ndpublishing.com

For a complete catalog write to:

New Directions

80 Eighth Avenue

New York, NY 10011